Color.

Look and say. Match.

Story **Structure:** *It's …*
Vocabulary: colors

Connect the dots. Color and say.

2.

1.

3.

2.

1.

2.

3.

1.

2.

3.

Trace and say. Match.

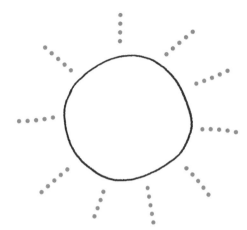

Smart topic **A rainbow**
Vocabulary: *rainy, sunny, rainbow*

Trace and say. Color.

Smart topic DVD A rainbow
Vocabulary: *rainy, sunny, rainbow*

Draw yourself and color.

Find the one that is different. Circle and say.

   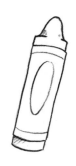

Say and match. Color.

2 •

1 •

3 •

Kindergarten DVD **Question:** *What can you see?*
Vocabulary: *book bag, crayon, book*

Unit 2

Look and say. Match.

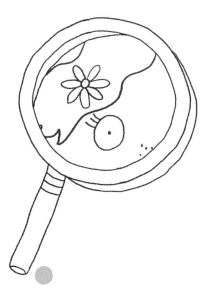

New words
Vocabulary: *mommy, daddy, brother, sister*

9

Look and circle 4 differences in Picture 2. Say.

Story **Structure:** *I want my …*
Vocabulary: family

Trace and say.

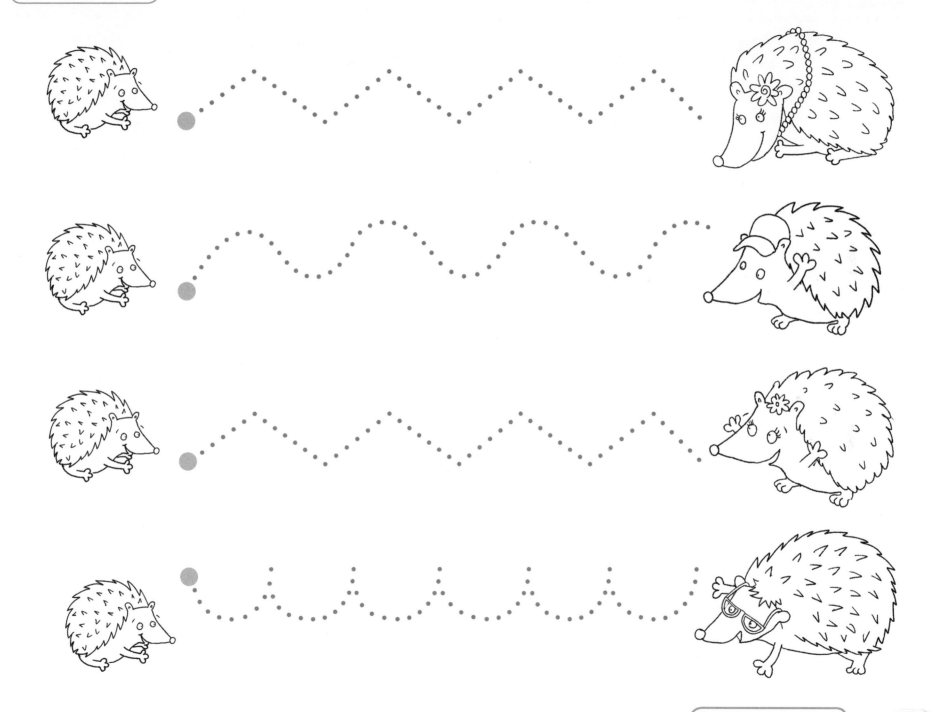

Match and trace. Say.

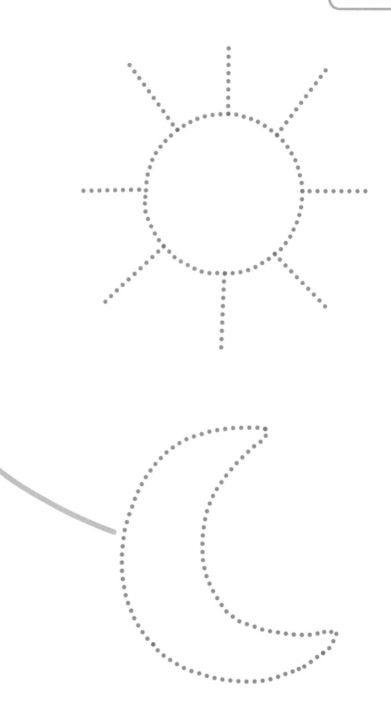

Smart topic Day and night
Vocabulary: *day, night*

Color the dots yellow. Find and say.

Draw yourself. Draw a sun or a moon. Color.

Review Lessons 1–6

Look and count. Circle the numbers.

1 2 ③

1 2 3

1 2 3

1 2 3

Find the same. Circle and say.

Kindergarten DVD **Question:** *Who takes you to school?*
Vocabulary: *grandma, grandpa*

Unit 3

Look and trace. Say.

New words
Vocabulary: *head, body, arms, legs*

Look and circle 4 differences in Picture 2. Say.

Story **Structure:** *Look at my …*
Vocabulary: body

Match and trace.

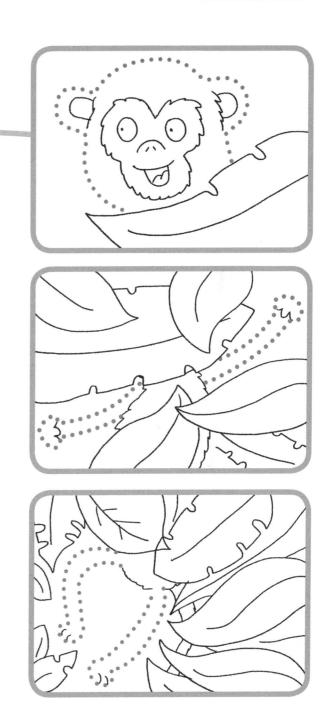

Trace and say. Count and match.

Smart topic Face
Vocabulary: *nose, mouth, eyes, ears*

Count and circle.

 1 2 3

 1 2 3

 1 2 3

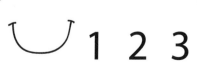 1 2 3

Trace and draw yourself.

Review Lessons 1–6

Trace and draw. Say.

Kindergarten DVD **Actions**
Vocabulary: *Stand up! Sit down! Walk!*

23

Look and match. Say.

Kindergarten DVD **Structure:** *Let's all …*
Vocabulary: *Stand up! Sit down! Walk!*

Unit 4

Look and say. Match.

New words
Vocabulary: *tortoise, dog, rabbit, fish*

Look and say. Match.

Story **Structure:** *Be quiet!*
Vocabulary: animals

Remember. Follow the path. Say.

Look and match the next one. Say.

Smart topic Farm animals
Vocabulary: *sheep, horse, cow, chicken*

Count and match.

Find and say. Circle. Draw your favorite animal.

Review   Lessons 1–6

Say, trace, and match.

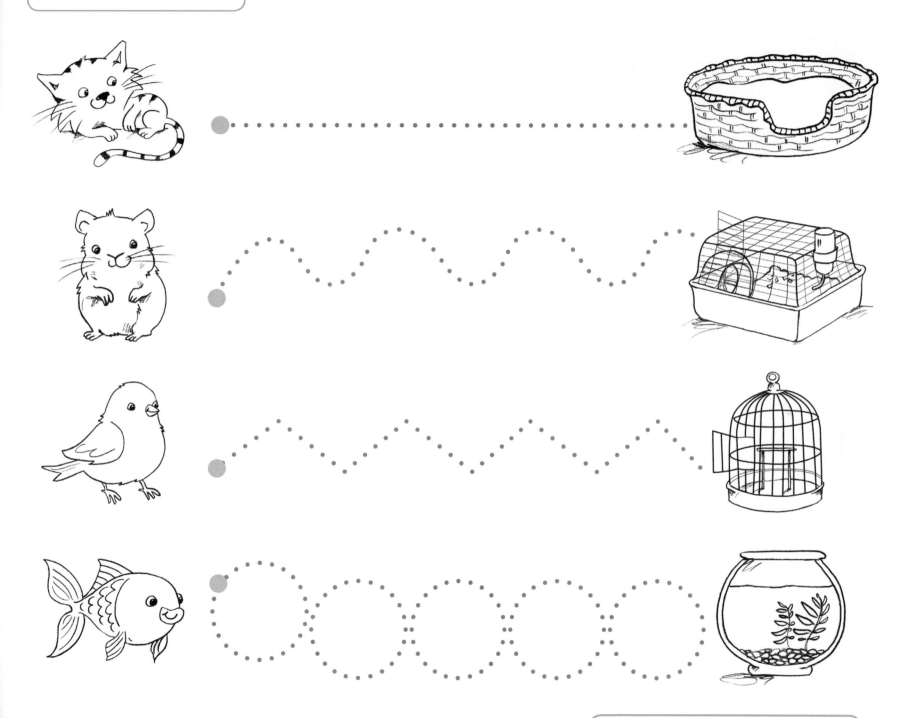

Look and circle the next one. Say.

Kindergarten DVD **Question:** *What's your favorite pet?*
Vocabulary: *hamster, bird, kitten*

Unit 5

Look and say. Match.

New words
Vocabulary: *mailman, doctor, teacher, cleaner*

33

Remember. Color the story characters.

Story **Structure:** *They see … / We see …*
Vocabulary: jobs

Remember. Connect the dots.

Trace and say. Match.

Smart topic Feelings
Vocabulary: *tired, excited, sad, happy*

Circle the one that is different.

Look and say. Match.

Review Lessons 1–6

Say. Draw the paths.

Look and circle. Say.

Kindergarten DVD **Question:** *Who helps us at school?*
Vocabulary: *lunch lady, secretary, teacher*

Unit 6

Look and trace. Say.

New words
Vocabulary: *teddy bear, car, doll, dinosaur*

Look and circle 4 differences in Picture 2. Say.

Story **Structure:** *Can I have a …?*
Vocabulary: toys

Draw yourself and say.

Look and circle the next one. Say.

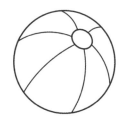  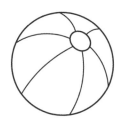   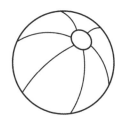

Smart topic Outdoor toys
Vocabulary: *bike, ball, scooter, jump rope*

Count and circle.

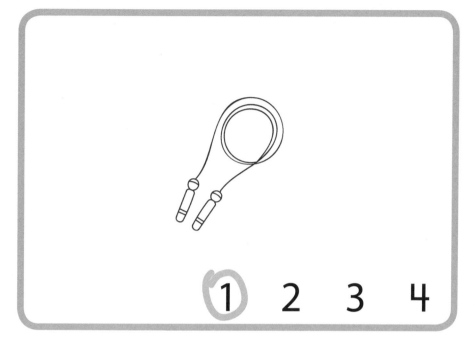

1 2 3 4

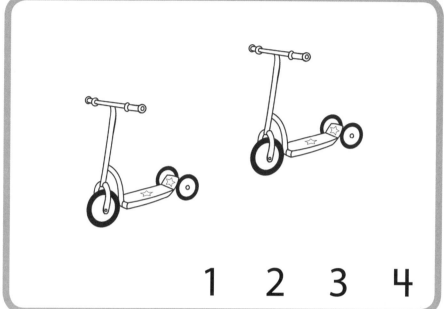

1 2 3 4

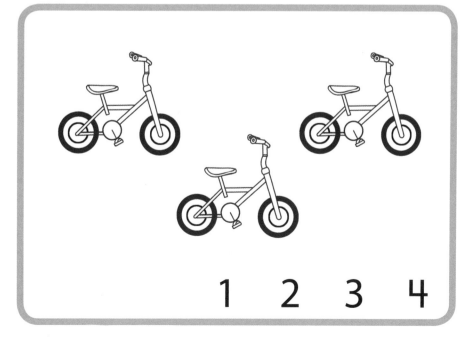

1 2 3 4

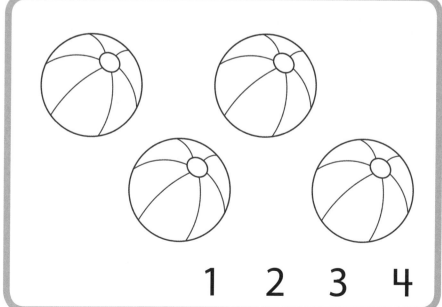

1 2 3 4

Look and say. Circle  if you like the toy.

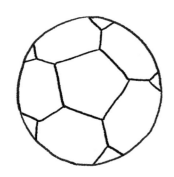

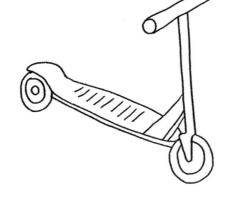

Review Lessons 1–6

Find the same. Circle and say.

  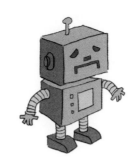  

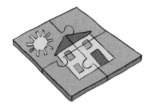    

Count and color.

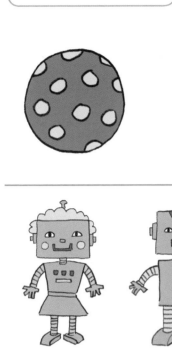  1 2 3 4

    1 2 3 4

 1 2 3 4

 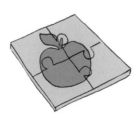 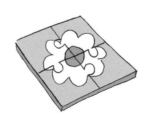 1 2 3 4

Kindergarten DVD **Question:** *What's your favorite toy?*
Vocabulary: *truck, puzzle, robot*

Unit 7

Trace and color. Say.

Remember. Follow the path and say.

Story **Structure:** *The baker needs … / I need …*
Vocabulary: food

Trace. Match and say.

Story **Structure:** *The baker needs … / I need …*
Vocabulary: food

Look and circle the next one. Say.

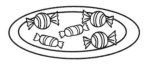     

Smart topic Healthy food
Vocabulary: *fish, candy, salad, cookies*

Count and circle.

 1 2 3 4 5

 1 2 3 4 5

 1 2 3 4 5

1 2 3 4 5

1 2 3 4 5

 1 2 3 4 5

Look and say. Match.

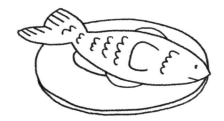

Say *hot* or *cold*. Draw yourself.

Count and match.

1

2

3

4

5

Kindergarten DVD   **Question:** *What are you having today?*
Vocabulary: *hot lunch, cold lunch*

Unit 8

Trace and match. Color.

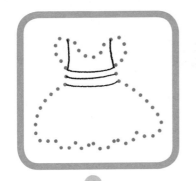
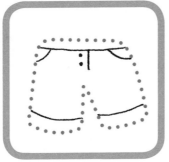
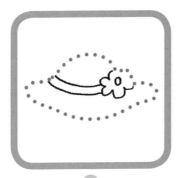

New words
Vocabulary: *dress, shorts, hat, T-shirt*

Look and circle 5 differences in Picture 2. Say.

Story **Structure:** *I'm wearing (a) …*
Vocabulary: clothes

Look and say. Match.

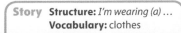

Look and color. Say.

1 green   2 blue   3 red   4 yellow

Smart topic Clothes
Vocabulary: *pants, sweater, jacket, umbrella*

Count and match. Color.

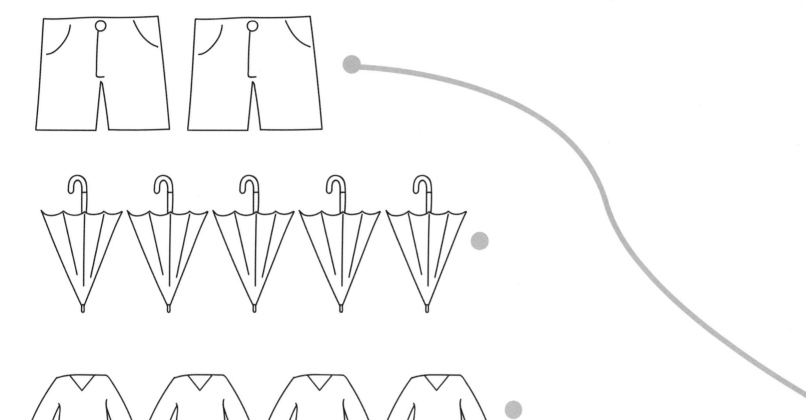

5

3

2

4

Look and say. Match.

Review Lessons 1–6

Look and circle the next one. Say.

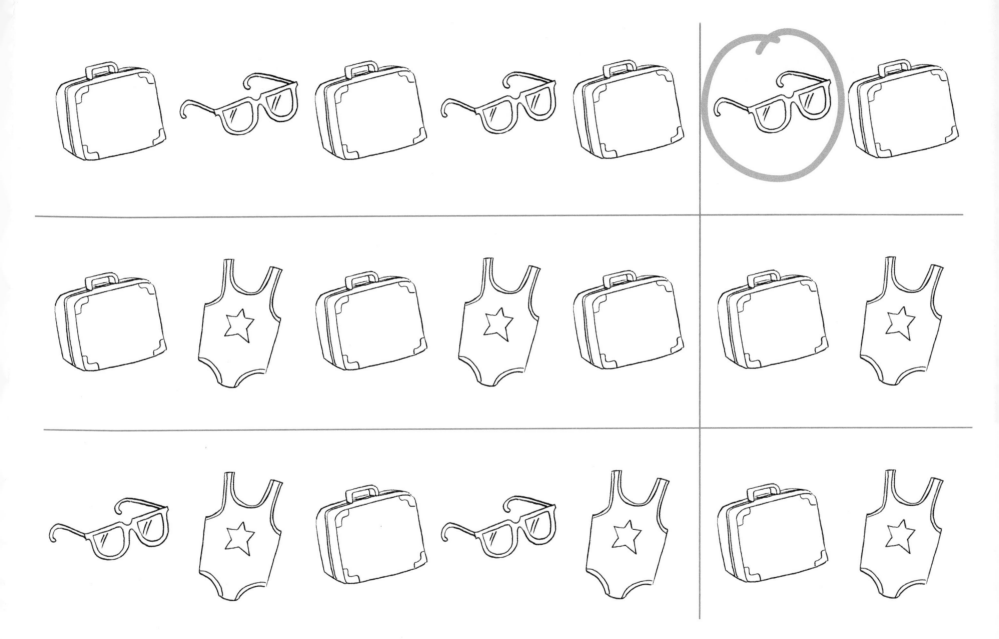

Trace. Connect the dots.

2

3

1

4

Kindergarten DVD **Question:** *What are you taking on vacation?*
Vocabulary: *suitcase, sunglasses, bathing suit*